Momma Said
101

Carolyn Hannah
Sharon Campbell Starks

ISBN 978-1-68570-793-4 (paperback)
ISBN 978-1-68570-794-1 (digital)

Christian Faith Publishing
832 Park Avenue
Meadville, PA 16335
www.christianfaithpublishing.com

Verses marked TLB, KJV, and GNT are taken from The Living Bible, the King James Version of the Bible, and the Good News Translation, respectively. Copyright © 1971. Used by permission of Tyndale House Publishers Inc., Wheaton, Illinois, 60189. All rights reserved.

Printed in the United States of America

Contents

Think back. Can you remember what
your momma used to say?
Well, as you begin to turn these pages,
trust us it'll all start to come back!
Write us and let us know.

From the Authors

G rowing up we both wondered why our moms were always repeating what we thought were some old phrase, that is until we became "moms".

As we have grown in our spiritual journey, we now realize those sayings are intertwined with the word of God.

Now that we look back, we are thankful for all those phrases our moms, said.

We believe your reading of this book "old phrases" will become clear to you as well.

1. A burden shared is a load lifted.
Many hands make light work.

> *Bear ye one another's burdens, and so fulfil the law of Christ. (Galatians 6:2 KJV)*
> *Two can accomplish more than twice as much as one, for the results can be much better. (Ecclesiastes 4:9 TLB)*

- Working as a team is more productive when all individuals involved have the same goal.

Am I my brother's keeper? We are only as strong as the weakest member of the body is. It is my responsibility to help when I know there is a need.

Think about this: What happens when you smash your finger? Doesn't it make your whole body feel bad?

Here are just a few ways we can help each other:

- Open the door for ladies and our seniors.
- Offer a ride to someone who needs it.
- Take time to call or visit those who might be sick or homebound.
- Be a good listener.

2. A closed mouth is never fed.

The lips of the righteous feed many; but fools die for want of wisdom (Proverbs 10:21 KJV)

- Others cannot read your mind; you must ask for help when you need it.

It seems like yesterday that I heard my mother say this to me.

One vivid memory is that of me doing everything I could to make my finances meet the needs of me and my girls and finally accepting the fact that it was not enough money.

I complained to my mom that life was a struggle. I just didn't understand why I had to experience financial woes and, no matter how I cut corners, I didn't have enough to pay bills and get basic needs for the girls and myself. She replied with this, "Tell me what you need if you want my help."

3. A drunken mind speaks a sober heart.

> *Wine gives false courage; hard liquor leads to brawl; what fools men are to let it master them, making them reel drunkenly down the street. (Proverbs 20:1 TLB)*
>
> *Whoso keepeth his mouth and his tongue keepeth his soul from troubles. (Proverbs 21:23 KJV)*

- When you are intoxicated, you often do and say things that you would not do or say if you were sober.

Needless to say, whenever I heard this saying, I rolled my eyes and sucked my teeth and thought how would my mother know about this. I had never seen her drunk.

Well, many years later, I have seen a few people "drunk." Their personality changed. And those who had appeared timid, mild-mannered, and easygoing became loud, boisterous, and very talkative. Others who had been strong-willed and set in their ways became "crybabies," indecisive, and so accommodating. The drink had truly affected their moods.

4. A friend sticks closer than a brother.

A man that hath friends must show himself friendly: and there is a friend sticketh closer than a brother. (Proverbs 18:24 KJV)

- True friends are a gift from God. They will always be in your heart and part of your life.
- We can't choose our family. We do have a choice of those we call "friends."
- Friends see us for who we are and like us anyway.

There is no doubt that family is important. However, there's nothing like a friend.

A friend obviously is someone you know: How many of us still have a friend we've known since kindergarten, someone we made mud pies with? Do you have any friend from high school, someone maybe you double-dated with or shopped with? Maybe you still have a friend from college, someone who helped you study for that crucial exam.

A friend is someone you can trust, someone who, no matter how much they are offered, will not betray your confidence. A friend is someone who will tell you the truth and not hurt your feelings in the process. A friend is someone who allows you the spotlight and is happy for you, instead of being envious of you.

A friend is someone you can share your life with, and they will know exactly what to say or not say.

It is possible to have several friends, but most of us would be happy to have just "one." If you are looking for a friend, I have just the one for you. I invite you to try Jesus as your friend. He'll always be there for you. You can tell Him anything. He'll pick you up and turn your life around. Best of all, He'll never leave you alone. He'll stick with you, closer than a brother.

5. A lie runs; the truth walks but gets there.

> *Truth shall spring out of the earth; and righteousness shall look down from heaven. (Psalm 85:11 KJV)*

- Bad news (gossip) is usually heard before good news. Words of encouragement are far more useful.

Far too many times, I've witnessed this saying in action. It's our nature to impress and to persuade others. It's our nature to put our own spin on information we receive and pass on to others.

These thoughts, together, usually result in the truth being stretched and changed and fantasy added on to gain others' interest.

Keep in mind that we listen and retain information that sounds good and is appealing. We add our own beliefs, and this information is quicker to get passed on (rumors).

Information that is fact, is easily verified, and has no room for change usually isn't too exciting. And after all, we can all access this when necessary; it just isn't part of everyday conversation (just not juicy enough).

This information is slow to reach us. We get the truth after all is said and done.

6. Actions speak louder than words; or put up or shut up.

Talk no more so very proudly, let not arrogance come from your mouth: for the Lord is a God of knowledge, and by Him actions are weighed. (1 Samuel 2:3 KJV)

- If you do not do what you say you will, then your words have no meaningful value. It would be wiser to say nothing at all.

Although words are important, equally as important are the actions that follow the words. Some people will say anything to get their point across or make them believable.

We as Christians say we believe but often fail to act on those "beliefs." We must put our faith into action in order for the words to have meaning.

- Believe God to give you a promotion. Sleep with the boss just in case.

One way of showing our faith would be to start taking classes in preparation for the new assignment.

7. All talk, no action.

Prove all things; hold fast to that which is good. (1 Thessalonians 5:21 KJV)

• Constant bragging without actual results is self-defeating. What the "eyes" can see is more believable.

Often, while I was growing up, my mother would say: "Look around you and see for yourself. People will tell you anything, but do they follow through with it?" If they told you one thing and did another, that lets you know they are all talk and no action.

Momma would go on to say: "If a person tells you about their plan but never takes steps toward getting it done, they are all talk and no action."

8. Be careful what you wish for; you just might get it.

> *Be not ye therefore like unto them: for your Father knoweth what things ye have need of, before ye ask. (Matthew 6:8 KJV)*

- When we fail to go to God with our request, we usually get what we asked for. What we asked for is not always what we need or what we really want.

I'm amazed, as I look back and remember my younger years, how often I heard this from my mother. Whenever I got into trouble and was punished, I would mumble my plan for my children (when I had them) or myself.

She would try to explain that I might plan, hope, or desire things to be different, but when I had my chance, I would see things differently.

What she was saying to me was we see the good and never realize that bad comes with it.

We want what we want when we want it and how we want it. Once we get what we thought we wanted, it is then we realize that there is more to it than what we wished for.

9. Big things come in small packages.

> *Here is another of his illustrations: "This Kingdom of Heaven is like a tiny mustard seed planted in a field. It is the smallest of all seeds, but becomes the largest of plants, and grows into a tree where birds can come and find shelter." (Matthew 13:31–32 TLB)*

- It's not the physical size that counts, rather what is in our heart. Faith the size of a mustard seed can move mountains.
- One of the best examples I can offer is David vs. Goliath.

I must thank my siblings for the training I received in this area as I was growing up. I am the fourth of five children and the smallest of the bunch. Rarely chosen to be a part of the group (after all, I was the baby), what could I do?

Feelings of loneliness and rejection would sometimes cloud my day. It was at those times that my mother would comfort me with these very words: "Big things come in small packages." Not really knowing what she meant but trusting in what she said, I committed those words to memory.

Whenever times were tough in school or at work or in general, my thoughts would somehow lead me back to the faith and inspiration of my mother. She is right. Big things do come in small packages!

10. **Birds of a feather flock together; or show me your friends, and I'll tell you about yourself.**

> *You can detect them by the way they act, just as you can identify a tree by its fruit. You need never confuse grapevines with thorn bushes or figs with thistles. (Matthew 7:16 TLB)*
>
> *Yes, the way to identify a tree or a person is by the kind of fruit produced. (Matthew 7:20 TLB)*

- Typically, "like-minded" people associate with each other. Having similar interests increases the depth of the friendship.

Food for thought:

Married and single people do not usually hang out together. Although there are some exceptions, you are usually more comfortable with those who are most like you.

Nonsmokers normally do not hang out with smokers. We do not like the smell (no offense).

Christians usually do not hang out in bars. The "spirit" we are looking for cannot be found in a bottle, can, or glass.

11. Blood is thicker than water.

So overflowing is His kindness toward us that he took away all our sins through the blood of his son, by whom we are saved. (Ephesians 1:7 TLB)

- All families experience differences, but in the end, commitment by family and friends is proven more beneficial.

Surely, every person who has siblings has heard this saying. As a sibling and as a parent, I have used this to encourage my children to work out their differences or to remember the connecting force they share.

I associate this saying with those who have siblings or parents who are often reminding them of the common connecting force between siblings. This saying is a reminder of what should bind family and relatives together. This saying solidifies what true blood relatives should abide by when there are conflicts and separations within families.

12. Bought sense is better than borrowed sense.

To be wise is as good as being rich; in fact, it is better. You can get anything by either wisdom or money, but being wise has many advantages. (Ecclesiastes 7:11–12 TLB)

• A personal experience provides understanding that cannot be gained through another person's experience.

This is one of my favorite sayings. Of course, I didn't like to hear it when I was growing up. My children, I'm sure, are sick of hearing me say it.

I understand my mother's point now. I couldn't learn from her mistakes or those of my siblings or friends. I had to experience it personally, by trial and error. Then I understood that when it's a bad experience, I don't go that route again and when it's a good experience, I go back for more.

13. Christians give Christianity a bad name.

For many shall come in my name, saying I am the Christ; and shall deceive many. (Matthew 24:5 KJV)

- Christianity is unconditional love. If all the Christians would actively practice this, we would have a far better world than the one we live in. Racism and hatred have no place in the life of a Christian.

We Christians can sometimes be intolerant people (certainly not a characteristic of Jesus).

Have you ever said one of the following?

- "Look at that dress she has on."
- "Can you believe they have drums and guitars in the church?"
- "Christian women do not wear pants and certainly not to church."
- "Did you hear how loud she was clapping?"
- "What's this 'praise and worship' thing all about?"
- "I don't know why she got the solo. She can't sing."

If one of the above describes you, just ask yourself if that was a thought or comment that a Christian should have.

14. Do unto others as you would have them do to you (but do it first).

> *Therefore all things whatsoever ye would that men should do to you, do ye even so to them: for this is the law and the prophets. (Matthew 7:12 KJV)*
> *Thou shalt love Thy neighbor as thyself. (Matthew 19:19b KJV)*

- Be the first to show an act of kindness, instead of expecting others to supply your need.

This means exactly what it says. If we honored it, how fewer tragedies would we have faced as a world, as a nation, as a race of people, or as individuals?

- We would not have suffered the "9/11" tragedy.
- Ms. Rosa Parks would never have been asked to give up her seat.
- Priests would not be resigning from their calling because of indiscretions.
- Mothers would not be abandoning their babies.
- Would we ever have known such a phrase as *road rage*?

These are only a few examples, but we are sure you can add to the list. Our question is, When will we stop adding examples and start removing some of them?

15. Do your best.

I know that there is no good in them, but for a man to rejoice, and do good in his life. (Ecclesiastes 3:12 KJV)

- When you do less than your best, you cheat yourself of achieving excellence.
- Why waste time doing the same job two or three times when you can do it right the first time?
- All anyone could ever ask of you is your best.

Are you doing your best?

Let's take a poll, looking back over the last year only: How often did you settle for less than your best?

- When you were in school, did you settle for Bs and Cs, knowing you should have gotten As?
- How often do you blame circumstances, as well as others (if he would have done this, then I could have…), when you don't get the results you are looking for?
- How much time have you wasted during the past year?

Time is winding down. Let's start *today* by doing our very best. Our best is what we and others expect of each other and what God expects from us.

16. Don't be the one to throw a rock and hide your hand.

> *Neither do men light a candle, and put it under a bushel, but on a candlestick; and it giveth light unto all that are in the house. (Matthew 5:15 KJV)*

- Take ownership of what you do, good or bad, and it will let those around you know your position.

This saying was spoken often as I grew up. I learned early in life that it did not matter if we were right or wrong when we participated in an act. Good or bad, we should acknowledge our part in the act.

Specifically, one of my sisters and a group of her friends were accused of disrespecting an adult in our neighborhood. When my mother confronted her about the neighbor's complaint, my sister not only admitted that she was the one doing the talking but corrected the adult's words with what she really said. My sister's words were even more disrespectful than reported. My mother punished her for what she said but thanked her for taking ownership for her behavior.

17. Don't bite off more than you can chew.

> *Unless you have extra cash on hand, don't countersign a note. Why risk everything you own? They'll even take your bed. (Proverbs 22:26–27 TLB)*

- Just say, "No."
- It is unwise to accept more responsibility than you are capable of handling.

This reminds me of the old saying, "Keeping up with the Joneses." Well, who are the Joneses? Furthermore, who said we should keep up with them? And if everyone is keeping up with them, whom are they keeping up with?

For instance:

- Sister Jones buys a new dress every week; therefore, you have to buy a new suit every week.
- Sister Jones buys an Envoy; you buy an Escalade.
- Sister Jones buys a three-bedroom house; you buy a five-bedroom house.

Of course, we could go on and on, but we're sure you get the idea.

18. Don't bite the hand that feeds you.

Don't be quick tempered, that is being a fool.
(Ecclesiastes 7:9 TLB)

• It is ill-advised to anger those you depend on.

We are blessed when we make wise choices instead of rash decisions.

- If you are living at home, rent-free (adult children), eating whatever you want, why would you have a problem helping out with chores?
- An employee with good benefits: The boss asks you to do something outside of your normal job function, and you feel it is beneath you. In the words of T. D. Jakes, "I'm still on the clock."
- Tithing: Ten percent is all God asks. He allows us to keep the other 90 percent. Why do so many "Christians" have a problem with tithing?

19. Don't cut off your nose to spite your face.

Be ye angry and sin not: let not the sun go down upon your wrath. (Ephesians 4:26 KJV)

- Make decisions when you have taken time to think the situation through. (Count to ten, and consult God.) Don't make a decision in anger because you usually regret it once you have calmed down.

Pride often gets in our way, preventing us from getting what we want, when we want it, the way we want it. This often causes us to make irrational decisions that lead to hurt feelings and anger.

20. Don't do evil for evil; or two wrongs don't make a right.

> *Never pay back evil for evil. Do things in such a way that everyone can see you are honest clear through. (Romans 12:17 TLB)*
> *God is more pleased when we are just and fair than when we give gifts. (Proverbs 21:3 TLB)*

- Just because someone has wronged you does not give you an excuse for bad behavior (no matter how tempting it might be). File it as something for Jesus to handle and leave it alone.

Choices, choices:

- Someone cuts you off while driving. Do you return the favor?
- Your mate cheated. Do you use this as an excuse to do the same?
- You find out someone lied to you. Do you turn around and lie to them?

Clearly, the first person is wrong in the above situations. You have a decision to make. Do you sink to their level, or do you rise above?

The best example is Jesus dying on the cross. He was judged falsely and sentenced to death. Instead of being angry and retaliating, He simply said in Luke 23:34, "Father, forgive them, for they know not what they do."

This is the only example we should ever need.

The *choice* is *yours*.

21. Don't let your right hand know what your left hand is doing.

> *But when you do a kindness to someone, do it secretly—don't tell your left hand what your right hand is doing. (Matthew 6:3 TLB)*

- Everyone you come in contact with should not know everything you do.

Whom do we seek to impress? Are we seeking to bring glory to God or to ourselves?

If we are fortunate enough to give donations, that's great! However, until we give the way the "widow woman" gave (all she had), we shouldn't be so quick to pat ourselves on the back.

All we have comes from God. So, if we are giving on behalf of the Owner, why do we feel the need to boast?

22. Don't make promises you can't keep.

It is far better not to say you'll do something than to say you will and then not do it. (Ecclesiastes 5:5 TLB)

• Promises are often made to impress others or to make us look good. If you know you will not be able to fulfill a promise, don't make it.

Most of us have said this on at least one occasion, "Lord, if You get me out of this, I'll... (you finish the sentence)." You knew you didn't mean it, 'cause you'd probably repeated that phrase several times before.

What would happen if God decided to collect on just one of those promises? Let this serve as a warning: sooner or later, He will collect.

23. Don't put off tomorrow what you can do today.

> *Withhold not good from them to whom it is due, when it is in the power of thine hand to do it. Say not unto thy neighbour, Go, and come again, and tomorrow I will give; when thou hast it by thee. (Proverbs 3:27–28 KJV)*

- We have today. Accomplish all that you can. Tomorrow is not promised.

Today is unlike any other day; we have a responsibility to make the most of it. We often put things as well as people off, believing that we have all the time in the world. Looking back at the events of September 11, 2001 and more recently the COVID Pandemic, we are reminded that we should not take life for granted. We never know how much time we have.

Here are just a few more reminders:

- The shutoff notice you always think you have more time to pay.
- A potential college student who got his paperwork in on the day of the deadline, but all the scholarship money was gone.
- A job applicant who responds to an ad on Thursday and finds out the position was filled on Monday.
- A workaholic, whose favorite line was "I'll rest tomorrow," becomes the victim of a heart attack.
- A smoker who promised to quit tomorrow. Tomorrow came, but so did lung cancer.

Get the point? Whatever it is, do it today; tomorrow is not promised.

24. Don't throw stones if you live in a glass house.

> *So when they continued asking him, he lifted up himself, and said unto them, "He that is without sin among you, let him first cast a stone at her." (John 8:7 KJV)*

- We have all sinned and fallen short. I should not blame or ridicule you, when I have done (in some cases, still doing) the same thing.

Whenever we point at someone else, we should always remember that there are three fingers pointing back at us.

If we spent our time taking care of our own flaws, we would not have time to point at anyone else's. Certainly, if others wanted to, they could point out the flaws in us.

25. Don't trouble, trouble, until trouble troubles you.

Although affliction cometh not forth of the dust, neither doth trouble spring out of the ground. (Job 5:6 KJV)

• Avoid people and places that cause you to respond negatively.

Ladies, why would you go over to your "baby daddy's house" uninvited?

"I'm going to my baby daddy's house, because the baby needs some Pampers."

We all know you are checking up on him and the end result is unnecessary trouble.

26. Empty wagons make a lot of noise.

Therefore doth Job open his mouth in vain; he multiplieth words without knowledge. (Job 35:16 KJV)

- When those who lack knowledge speak, it sounds just like the rattles of an empty wagon (just a lot of noise).

We all have at least one relative or friend who has the KIA (know-it-all) syndrome. They know everything about everything. They've been everywhere and done everything.

If you would look closely at their lives, you would probably see that they are some very sad and lonely people.

- Uncle Cornbread talks loud enough for the next-door neighbor to hear.
- The bourgeois sister usually spends Saturday nights home alone.

Examine those who always have something to say; you might be surprised at what you find.

27. Every shut eye is not sleep and every goodbye is not gone.

Keep alert and pray. Otherwise temptation will overpower you. For the spirit indeed is willing, but how weak the body is! (Matthew 26:41 TLB)

- Familiarize yourself with places and people on a regular basis. Preparedness prevents delayed reactions.

Another of my favorite sayings!

- Through the years, I've witnessed this over and over. Someone leaves the room; and those left start to make comments, good or bad, only to look and see the person just outside the door or reentering the room, having heard what was said.
- A person is at a gathering with others and apparently sleeping. A few whispered comments are made about the person, and as others look over, that person is now awake and has heard everything.

Not sleep and not yet gone.

28. Everything happens for a reason; or there is a time and place for everything.

> *There is a right time for everything. (Ecclesiastes 3:1 TLB)*
> *Let all things be done decently and in order. (1 Corinthians 14:40 KJV)*

- We all struggle with this, young and old alike. We always want to know "Why me?", "Why this?", or "Why now?"
- Recognize when to be serious and when to have fun; both are equally important.

In the midst of a storm, if we would remember that God never leaves or forsakes us, it would have a calming effect on our spirits. We would then be open to receive the blessing from the storm.

- The reason you lost your job might be for you to be ready to receive a better one God has in store for you.
- The reason you got sick: your body might have been telling you it needed a rest, and you ignored the warning signs.
- The reason tragedy strikes: free will.

The time is now. With your free will, choose God.

29. Everything old is new again; or the more things change, the more they stay the same.

> *The thing that hath been, it is that which shall be; and that which is done is that which shall be done: and there is no new thing under the sun. (Ecclesiastes 1:9 KJV)*
>
> *Jesus Christ the same yesterday, today and forever. (Hebrews 13:8 KJV)*

• The more things change, the more they stay the same.

My granny used to say, "Hold on to the articles of clothes or shoes you really like. Before you know it, they'll be in style again."

Haven't you heard the younger generation say, "It's a new millennium." This is true. However, basic morals and values should not change.

- Afros were hot in the 1970s, and they are hot again.
- Bell-bottom pants were hot when I was growing up. And, now, years later, they are hot again.

30. Find a penny. Pick it up. All day you'll have luck.

For thou shalt eat the labour of thine hands:
happy shalt thou be, and it shall be well with thee.
(Psalm 128:2 KJV)

- Slow down; take time to notice the small things in life. If you take care of the small ones, the big ones will not seem so big.

How many times have you been in such a hurry to do something that later you couldn't remember the details?

For me, this saying is a reminder of the small stuff that appears to have no major impact on our lives or is not valued or appreciated enough.

- Imagine finding one penny every day of your life for ten years. That's $3,650! Now does that make you appreciate the small things in your life?

Slow down and collect your penny each day. It is valuable.

31. Go to bed with dogs; you'll get up with fleas.

Be not deceived; evil communications corrupt good manners. (1 Corinthians 15:33 KJV)

- You cannot continue to associate with evil without eventually becoming evil or doing evil deeds.

It seemed that every time I went out on a date, this was one of the few sayings my mother said before I left the house.

I now realize that my mother was saying, "Be careful what you do and whom you do it with."

Associate with people with ill manners and bad reputations, and eventually you become a part of them.

32. God doesn't like ugly, and pretty doesn't please Him.

The Lord blesses good men and condemns the wicked. (Proverbs 12:2 TLB)

• It is not how you look on the outside but what is in your heart that really counts.

This saying reminds me of those we call "tattletales." No matter how much we've done wrong, we are always willing to go tell on someone else (hypocrite). I'm not saying we should condone wrong. I'm saying that we should clean the skeletons in our own closet before cleaning those from someone else's. It is up to each individual to get right with God. We cannot do that for them.

For all the pretty people: no matter how physically attractive you may be or how good you think you are, we are all "dirt" in the eyes of God.

33. Haste makes waste.

Dear brothers, don't ever forget that it is best to listen much, speak little, and not become angry. (James 1:19 TLB)

- Don't make quick decisions.
- Think about your desired outcome. Consult God and plan accordingly.

We all have a hundred examples of where this is true.

- The time when you were late for work and got a ticket because you were speeding
- How about the time you were in line at the airport and forgot your ticket
- How about the time you were at the counter ready to pay and found that you had no money because you forgot your wallet
- What about the time you were baking a cake and forgot to put in a certain ingredient
- What about when you lost some money in an investment you made (sounded legitimate) but failed to check it out first

All these examples show that with just a little more time and preparation, the time that was wasted could have been avoided.

34. He may not come when you want, but He's always on time.

> *The righteous cry, and the Lord hearth, and deliverEth them out of all their troubles. (Psalms 34:17 KJV)*

- Our timing is not God's timing. Just because we think we are ready to handle a situation doesn't mean that we are.

What we learn from this saying is God sees the big picture. We are often using time schedules to meet goals. Although we want instant resolution or response, God knows better than we do when we actually need it.

We may think we need a new job right now, and we are praying and believing for it right now. Yet the job is not given to us for weeks, months, or even years later.

No matter when we are blessed, we should be receptive.

35. He who hesitates is lost.

> *For God says, "Your cry came to me at a favorable time, when doors of welcome were wide open. I helped you on a day when salvation was being offered." Right now God is ready to welcome you. Today he is ready to save you. (2 Corinthians 6:2 TLB)*

- Don't spend a lot of time planning and preparing for what you have no control over. (When the spirit says move, then move.)

Obviously, there are some instances where a slight hesitation is advisable:

- Before driving through a green light that has just changed
- Not judging a situation or person before all the facts are known

Think of this as the one that got away:

- Looking back over your life, can you remember that special someone you wish you would have hooked up with? Maybe out of anger he/she did or said something you could not forgive them for; or maybe you did or said something, and you wouldn't say you were sorry. Time passed, you both moved on with your lives, but something nagged until one of you looked the other person up. What you found was that the other person was now happily married, involved, or just unavailable.
- Maybe you had a great idea that you just sat on. Years later, someone else not only had that idea but developed it and made a fortune.

The time is now. God saves the lost, so there is no need to hesitate.

36. Honesty is the best policy.

God knows we are honest, but I want everyone else to know it too. That is why we have made this arrangement. (2 Corinthians 8:21 TLB)

- Honesty builds character and trust. What type of a relationship can you have with someone if you do not trust them?

Many years of hearing and saying this to my children has resulted in me or them finishing this thought after the word *honesty* is spoken.

We all have difficulty with this saying because we don't believe it. When honesty results in hurting another or brings about a challenge or confrontation, it is unsettling. Yet, if we reflect on this saying, we will respect and trust more easily those who have consistently been honest with us.

37. I can show you better than I can tell you.

Yea a man say, Thou hast faith, and I have works: shew me thy faith without works, and I will show thee my faith with works. (James 2:18 KJV)

- Respect is earned, not given. What I do is far more important than anything I could ever say. My life should be an example of that which I speak.

As children, we were willing to help others, quick to show our capabilities. As adults, we often tell people one thing and then do another.

However, most of us look at others' deeds or actions as proof of what they have said.

Sometimes acceptance is only possible when we are observed doing what we say or living in a way that is Christlike when we say we are followers of Christ.

38. Idle minds/hands are the devil's workshop.

Yet we hear that some of you are living in laziness, refusing to work, and wasting your time gossiping. (2 Thessalonians 3:11 TLB)

- Develop goals, focus your thoughts, and aim for the stars. Too much unsupervised time allows you to get into trouble.

My mother taught us early in life that keeping busy prevents us from getting into trouble.

I can honestly say that I am seldom without pen and paper, jotting down thoughts, making notes for future plans. My mind is busy with thankful thoughts and reflections of the past.

The goal of this saying is to stay mindful of our own purpose, goal, or plan, not busy in others' affairs.

39. If at first you do not succeed, try again; or practice makes perfect.

Hope deferred maketh the heart sick: but when the desire cometh, it is like a tree of life. (Proverbs 13:12 KJV)

- If everything were handed to us, we would never know the value of work or the purpose of faith. Work helps to build our character and strengthen our faith.

Many times I had to re-mop a floor or remake a bed. Why? Because I was in a hurry and did not do it right the first time.

Little did I know that my parents were teaching me necessary problem-solving skills that I would need later in life. The lesson was not never to make a mistake but to have the fortitude to correct the mistake.

The following tasks take a lot of practice:

- Learning to walk
- Learning to drive
- The art of singing a note just right
- Making a free throw / scoring a goal
- Closing a sale

40. If all your friends jump off a bridge, are you going to jump too?

Blessed is the man that walketh not in the counsel of the ungodly, nor standeth in the way of sinners, nor sitteth in the seat of the scornful. (Psalm 1:1 KJV)

• The person you view as a mentor or role model is a leader for you in some aspects of your life. Consider carefully where they are leading you. Is it some place you really want to go?

The choice is not always ours, but we are all leaders in our respective lives. And as such, it is our responsibility to set a good example for those who follow us.

You are a leader if you are any of the following:

- Pastor
- Father/mother
- Teacher/coach
- Sister/brother
- Uncle/aunt
- Mentor
- CEO/president
- Supervisor / team leader
- Governor/mayor
- Senator/representative
- Policeman/fireman
- Lawyer/doctor

The list goes on. Hopefully you understand by now.

As a follower, choose your leader in such a manner that, should you need to make that jump, your landing will be a solid one, solid like a rock, instead of sinking sand.

41. If I can get up and go to work, every able body in the house is going to go to work or some place.

For even when we were with you, this we commanded you, that if any would not work, neither should he eat. (2 Thessalonians 3:10 KJV)

Momma was letting us know that we couldn't just sit around or sleep all day. We needed to make some type of effort, be it school or work, and it was our choice.

We live in a society that is full of contradictions, and we constantly contradict ourselves. Or we become enablers.

- Some of our teens of today feel that we owe them something. They feel they should live by their own rules, in their parents' home.
- We have another group of kids who live at home and do work but do not contribute to the family and really have nothing to show for their labor.

Parents, aunts, uncles, if either of the above categories fits, you are not doing yourself or your children any favors. We owe it to the younger generation to teach them responsibility and leadership skills. If at any time we are unsure as to what to do, all we need to do is find out what Jesus would do. He has all the answers.

42. If the shoe fits, wear it.

A trap doesn't snap shut unless it is stepped on; your punishment is well deserved. (Amos 3:5 TLB)

- Don't worry about things that do not concern you.

I once heard someone say, "You should not be caught standing over a dead person with a smoking gun in your hand."

No one, especially a Christian, should have a "just fired gun" in his or her hand (unless it is within the scope of your job), standing over a dead person.

The first impression of anyone who sees you would be that you fired the gun (the shoe fits). However, if you are not standing over the body holding the gun and you did not fire it, the shoe would not fit.

In other words, don't go places and do things you know you shouldn't do. Then you will not have to worry about the shoe fitting.

43. If you can't beat them, join them.

> *Behold I stand at the door, and knock: if any man hear my voice, and open the door, I will come in to him, and will sup with him, and he with me. (Revelations 3:20 KJV)*

- To increase understandings, meet an individual on their level.

Sometimes to affect change, you must first change yourself. Change your thoughts, your opinion, and/or, sometimes, your attitude. This change will allow you to see the other person's point of view. Once this is done, you will be more effective because you now know both sides.

Jesus will not beat us into submission. We do that to ourselves. It is our choice to join Him and allow ourselves to be changed or go to "the school of hard knocks."

He's knocking. What's your answer? Will you join Him?

44. If you don't want to fall, don't walk in slippery places.

I screamed, "I am slipping Lord!" and he was kind and saved me. (Psalm 94:18 TLB)

- The Word of God is our safety net; as long as we are walking in it, we do not have to worry about the world's "slips." On the other hand, if we are outside of God's Word, we must watch for the cliffs—it's a long way down.

The first time I heard this saying, I found myself, days later, trying to figure it out. I finally went back to my friend's mother, and she explained. We all have choices, and when we make a choice, we assume the outcome.

If we know the history of a choice, why would we choose it if we know the outcome is going to be negative?

If you see a sign on the floor saying, "Slippery when wet," and it's wet at that moment, why would you walk on the floor?

45. It does not matter who did the crime. You're all gonna do the time.

Be with wise men and become wise. Be with evil men and become evil. (Proverbs 13:20 TLB)

- You are responsible for the friends you choose and the things you agree to do with them.

It's nothing better than a group of people getting together with a common goal in mind.

When it's positive and beneficial, it's great. However, if something goes wrong or events change without all parties' consent, anyone who's seen with the group will be held responsible.

It's a good idea to get all the facts, to know the goal or the plan and what the expected outcome is supposed to be, for it will affect everyone involved.

46. It'll all come out in the wash.

> *Not by works of righteousness which we have done, but according to his mercy he saved us, by washing off regeneration, and renewing of the Holy Ghost. (Titus 3:5 KJV)*

• Truth always wins in the end.

This saying has given me comfort more times than I dare to remember. Whenever a situation arose, in which I had done my best, given my all, and told the truth, yet the outcome had not been what I expected or wanted, this saying would come to mind.

The saying means that it will be revealed when the time is right and everything is examined. All the unnecessary stuff is removed, and all that is left is truth and righteousness.

47. It's okay for people to think you are a fool; just don't open your mouth and prove that you are.

He that is void of wisdom despiseth his neighbor: but a man of understanding holdeth his peace. (Proverbs 11:12 KJV)

• It's not important what others think of you but what you think of yourself.

How I wish I had understood this saying when I was a young adult. There were so many times when I just had to respond to what someone had said. It was not always negative or positive. I just had to say something. Often, what I said did not apply to the situation at all. As I reflect on those times, it really would have been to my advantage to think what I said but not to speak it. Even I realize some of my responses had to make the other person(s) realize I didn't have a clue about what was really being discussed. I've since learned that even when I know what's being talked about, I don't have to share my thoughts or opinion and confirm myself as a know-it-all or know-nothing-at-all about the discussion.

48. It's a mighty long road that never ends.

We know these things are true by believing not seeing. (2 Corinthians 5:7 TLB)

- We must accept that our time here on earth is not forever.

Whenever one of the five of us children received a lecture from my mother about something, we really thought we were getting away without (a long span of time) getting caught. This was my mother's way of telling us, "You may think this will last forever, but even the longest road will end at some point." The things we were sneaking around doing would eventually be known.

49. It's a mighty bad wind that never changes.

The disciples just sat there, awed! "Who is this," they asked themselves, "that even the winds and the sea obey him?" (Matthew 8:27 TLB)

- It does not matter how bad things look; God has the final say on how it will come to pass.

This saying has often brought me comfort. My understanding of this is that things get rough and, in fact, we will experience storms in our lives. Again, no matter how difficult or bad things may appear, God can change the situation.

It doesn't matter how bad things are, a change in every storm takes place, because God has the final say.

50. Keep your friends close, but keep your enemies closer.

Wounds from a friend are better than kisses from an enemy. (Proverbs 27:6 TLB)

• A true friend has your best interest at heart. An enemy causes trouble.

This saying has been one of the guiding forces in my life. I have established a very close friendship with only a few people, and we all have similar beliefs and ideologies about life. However, there are a few who are not my friends. But our paths crossed, and due to circumstances, we must interact. I sense their true colors, and I keep a close eye and ear (monitor) on their interactions in my life. That includes one-on-one contact with them, as well as distant involvement, to ensure it has a minimum impact on my life.

51. Let go and let God.

> Let him have all your worries and cares, for he is always thinking about you and watching everything that concerns you. (1 Peter 5:7 TLB)
>
> No dear brothers, I am still not all I should be but I am bringing all my energies to bear on this one thing: Forgetting the past and looking forward to what lies ahead. I strain to reach the end of the race and receive the prize for which God is calling us up to heaven because of what Christ Jesus did for us. (Philippians 3:13–14 TLB)

- This means just what it says. Give all our concerns and worries to God. We really can't do anything about them anyway.
- We'll never really know the freedom and love we could experience, or the power of God, until we learn to let go. If we are always worried or always trying to hold on to a child, an abusive relationship, a job, or anger, how will we ever be able to enjoy life?
- We must learn to lean and depend on the One Who can, Who will, and Who does take care of us. That someone is God. Let go and let Him handle it.

52. Loose lips sink ships.

There is no need for me to condemn you, you are condemned by every word you speak. (Job 15:6 GNT)

- Personal or confidential information shared with the wrong person could be disastrous.

I have witnessed confidential information being shared, and this saying immediately comes to mind. We all have shared something with someone we didn't want them to pass on, yet they did. Or we have passed on some information that we had promised to keep to ourselves. Either of those situations can result in someone being physically or emotionally hurt. Disaster looms when information is unwisely shared.

53. Mind your mouth.

Mind your manners.

> *There is no need for me to condemn you, you are condemned by every word you speak (Job 15:6 GNT)*

- Our actions lead to "consequences," which are sometimes positive as well as negative. Free will allows us to make that choice. Which will you choose?

Growing up, especially during the teenage years, I had the "talk too much" syndrome (like many of you, I'm sure) ☺. I thought I should be able to respond to my mother and grandmother during heated conversations. Well, I've learned that just because they asked me a question didn't mean I was supposed to answer it, especially not the way in which I answered it.

It's just like that with God. When He asks us a question, do you really think He needs an answer from us? What God is looking for (as were our parents) is whether or not we know what the answer is and how we will use the information.

"Mind your mouth or mind your manners" came as a warning not to take my behavior to the next level. It was also an opportunity to get myself in check before either of them had to. (You know Momma would too!)

54. Mind your own business.

Above all, my brothers, do not use an oath when you make a promise. Do not swear by heaven or by earth or by anything else. Say only "yes" when you mean yes, and "no" when you mean no, and then you will not come under God's judgement. (Proverbs 4:11 GNT)

- It is easy to get "caught up" in someone else's drama. This takes the focus away from us, putting our lives on hold. We must remember if we do not deal with reality, reality will deal with us.

This is not always an easy principle to follow. Oftentimes, others bring their issues to us. Once this is done, we have to decide if we should just listen or should we get involved. We can never know all of someone else's circumstances the way we know our own. When we offer opinions, often, it is based on incomplete information. This situation often leads to misjudgments, hurt feelings, etc. Involvement is sometimes necessary, but overall, "mind your own business" is a good principle to live by.

55. My word is my bond.

Say just a simple Yes I will or no I won't. Your word is enough. To strengthen your promise with a vow shows that something is wrong. (Matthew 5:37 TLB)

But above all things, my brethren, swear not, neither by heaven, neither by the earth, neither by an oath: but let your yea be yea; and your nay, nay; lest you fall into condemnation. (James 5:12 KJV)

• A written contract between two Christians should not be necessary; your word should be good enough.

- In biblical times, one person would give another person their sandal in the presence of witnesses to seal an agreement.
- In the early part of the 1900s, an agreement was sealed with a handshake.
- Today, we have prenuptial agreements and contracts to seal agreements, and we employ attorneys to keep us from living up to those agreements!

Shouldn't our word mean something? What is "your word" worth?

56. Never judge a book by its cover.

> *But the Lord said unto Samuel, look not on his countenance, or on the height of his stature: because I have refused him: for the Lord seeth not as man seeth; for man looketh on the outward appearance, but the Lord looketh on the heart. (1 Samuel 16:7 KJV)*
>
> *Judge not, that ye be judged. (Matthew 7:1 KJV)*

• Appearances can be deceiving.

Each time you have looked at a person who appeared different in dress, behavior, or appearance and thought negative, only to later find out that person was not what you thought when you first laid eyes on them, you passed judgment.

We have many examples of this being true:

- A caterpillar turns into a beautiful butterfly.
- The seemingly lifeless trees with bare branches give way to a springtime harvest full of leaves with vibrant colors.

These are but two of the many examples of how you cannot judge by outward appearances. The Bible is another example of not being able to judge a book by the cover. Once you begin to search its pages, you'll find it will answer any question that you might have.

Within the pages of the Bible, you'll find everything you need to know about living a healthy, prosperous, spiritual life. So many of us look to others to solve our problems when we need only open our "textbook."

This saying is a reminder that looks can be deceiving.

57. Never leave something for nothing.

Behold, I come quickly: hold fast which thou hast, that no man take thy crown. (Revelations 3:11 KJV)

- When you are sure of what you have, don't give it up for uncertainty.

- Have you ever changed jobs because of what someone else promised you (nothing in writing) or left a job with a well-known firm to join one that no one had ever heard of because of an increase in salary? Once you took the new job, you found out that the old one wasn't bad after all.
- Have you ever gotten into a relationship because your mate no longer listened to you or you felt they weren't "there" for you? Once you got into that new relationship, things changed. You went from house on the hill to hardly able to pay your bills.
- Have you ever gotten your feelings hurt at church and decided to stop going? So you turned your back on God (Who is your source for all things), instead of walking away from the situation.

Sometimes we get caught up in the moment, and we do not take the time to think a situation through. We tend to make decisions based on emotions rather than fact. Think about the "something" that you already have, before making a decision that could leave you with "nothing."

58. Once the rubber meets the road, you'll get busy.

Commit thy works to the Lord, and thy thoughts shall be established. (Proverbs 16:3 KJV)

- As long as our lives are in the planning stages, we are unable to account for them. Once deadlines are set, productivity increases, and then goals are soon achieved.

Another of my favorite sayings:

The message to be conveyed here is that when we are serious about achieving a goal and the deadline is soon approaching, we get busy working to meet that goal.

I recently said to my daughter (who had been working during the summer and supposedly saving to return to school) that she had less than a month to meet her savings goal. Her response was "The rubber has met the road, and I've got to get serious about saving my money to return to school."

59. One bad apple spoils the whole bunch.

But it takes only one wrong person among you to infect all the others. (Galatians 5:9 TLB)

- It only takes one person in a group with a negative attitude to have an effect on the others in the group.

This saying is a reminder that one person can enter a room or a group with an opinion that is negative or critical and share it, and before long, several others will accept and share that opinion and change the atmosphere for all.

- One disgruntled worker seeking revenge can ruin the peace of mind of all the other workers.
- One car accident at "rush hour" can affect thousands of others.

If you are at home or work, driving, or just standing in line, "teamwork" is the key to success!

60. Play with a dog; he'll lick your mouth. Play with a child; he'll sass you out.

> *Scolding and spanking a child helps him learn. Left to himself, he brings shame to his mother. (Proverbs 29:15 TLB)*

- Too much playing and fun without guidelines usually results in hurt feelings and embarrassment.

Every time I hear a child talking back or someone say their dog bit them, this saying immediately comes to mind. For me, it's a reminder that others lose respect for us when we fail to set the guidelines and demand respect.

We may play with our pet or have fun with our children, but it's important to know when to stop playing. When we fail to do so, a time will come when we will not have the respect or control of the pet or the child and find ourselves upset by their behavior.

61. Practice what you preach.

A good man is known by his truthfulness; a false man by deceit and lies. (Proverbs 12:17 TLB)

- Don't say one thing and then do something different. Always be willing to take your "own" advice.

Kids like to push or test the limits. So, parents, if you want your kids to respond in a certain way, you must first respond that way yourself.

Parents, you have one of the most important jobs there is. It is your responsibility to set the example for your child and not allow the latest basketball, football, or singing sensation to do it for you.

Adults, in general, are not off the hook. As adults we have a responsibility to act as adults. If we all took a minute, we would realize that someone is watching us, wanting to step into our shoes (walk like us, talk like us, and dress like us). Think about this. Whose shoes did you want to fill when you were a kid?

Kids are like little sponges; they soak up what's around them. Who and what are your kids soaking up?

With all this said, parents (adults), "practice what you preach."

62. Remember that you are going to need your hands to fan the flies more than once.

Be patient, therefore, brethren, until the coming of the Lord. Behold, the farmer waits for the precious fruit of the earth, patient over it until it receives the early and late rain. (James 5:7 KJV)

- Don't mistreat others. The one you mistreat may be the very one you'll need to help you later on in life.

This saying is simply a reminder that it's important to treat others in such a way that whenever you cross their paths, they will be receptive to you.

We should treat people right, because you may need the person you thought you were least likely to need.

We all need others in our lives continuously, and although we may forget minor encounters with others, everyone has a different perspective on how things happened.

63. Remember what makes you laugh will also make you cry.

Laughter cannot mask a heavy heart. When the laughter ends, the grief remains. (Proverbs 14:13 TLB)

- We will always have tears of joy along with tears of pain.

- Surely you can think about a time when things were going well and it brought you the pleasure of laughter. Perhaps, months later, things changed. What was once a happy event has now brought unrest and sadness.
- Births, as well as deaths, can provoke our emotions from one extreme to the other.

64. Right does right.

To do right honors God; to sin is to despise him. (Proverbs 14:2 TLB)

- It's okay to do what's right, even when it is not the popular thing to do.

Does wrong, ever, equal right? Do you really need to be told what's right and what's wrong?

How often do you question your choice?

When we allow the Holy Spirit to live in us and guide us, making right choices becomes second nature.

We can start right now by making the following "right choices":

- Children (of all ages), obey your parents.
- Mates, respect each other.
- Friends, respect other friends.
- Drivers, obey the rules of the road and be courteous to each other.
- Christians, submit to God.

It takes time to see the results of making right choices (especially after having made a series of wrong ones). I'm here to tell you it's worth it. Start right now, today, making right choices.

65. Say what you mean and mean what you say.

Death and life are in the power of the tongue: and they that love it shall bear the fruit thereof. (Proverbs 18:21 KJV)

- If we understood that there are consequences for the words we speak, maybe we would chose them more wisely.

We must guard our gates, especially our mouths. How does anything get done?

The process starts with a thought, but you must put your thoughts into words to take action.

The way we formulate our words will lead to success or failure. Do you realize that you (by your words) have a say in the outcome of your life?

How do you think you would feel if everything you said sounded like one of the following: "I feel bad," "I'm lonely," "I'm sad," and "Nothing good ever happens to me." Saying them enough times, you soon start to feel the way you've said you felt. How can you feel good if you are always saying how bad you feel? How can you be happy if you are always talking about things that make you sad? Try it for yourself, or take note of those around you. Within a short period of time, I think you will be able to prove this for yourself.

Christians, try this: "This is the day that the Lord has made, and I will rejoice and be glad." "I'm too blessed to be stressed." "I've never seen the righteous forsaken or His seed begging bread." Try it. If you repeat those and add some of your own, I believe you will have a life-changing experience. You'll look good, you'll feel great, and, with God's help, no force will be able to stop you!

66. Talk is cheap; it takes money to buy land.

Work brings profit; talk brings poverty. (Proverbs 14:23 TLB)

- "Follow-through" is important. It doesn't matter so much what you say. What matters most is what you do about what you've said.

This saying reminds me of "bragging rights" and free advice:

- Men:
  My car is faster than your car.
  My outfit is "phat," and yours isn't.
- Politicians:
  My record speaks for itself.
  If I'm elected, there will be no tax increases.
- Christians:
  If you get me out of this, Lord, I'll never do it again.
  You play "big shot" in front of the congregation but are unable to take care of business at home.

Talk is cheap and, sometimes, even free. The payment comes when the other person can actually depend on what you have said. Now, what if we had to pay for all the talk we could not prove or did not follow through on? What would your bill look like?

67. Talk long; you'll talk wrong every time.

*He that keepeth his mouth keepeth his life: but
he that openeth wide his lips shall have destruction.
(Proverbs 13:3 KJV)*

- Keep it simple. The less said, the better. This principle will
help eliminate gossip, as well as arguments and ill feelings.

We all have known someone who shared too much information, and as a result, those listening learned something that should not have been shared.

I've found that whenever I'd been caught in a situation that could result in my mother punishing me, I would try to explain what I thought would prevent punishment, only to end up telling her too much. The result would be my admitting to something that she didn't know and adding to my punishment.

For me, this saying supports what attorneys say to a witness being prepared for testimony: "When appropriate, give 'yes' or 'no' responses and short, simple answers. Never share information that is not asked for by the person questioning you."

68. Talking loud and saying nothing.

> *Let no corrupt communication proceed out of your mouths but that which is good to the use of edifying, that it may minister grace unto the hearers. (Ephesians 4:29 KJV)*

- When we speak without thinking, we get into more than we can handle.

We've all been in the midst of a crowd where we were hardly able to hear ourselves think. In the midst of the room, there's always one person who is talking loud enough for everyone to hear them. Have you ever wondered why? As you might have made your way over to them or tuned your ear to hear, what you found was that the person really didn't have anything useful to say.

In general, we all have a need to be acknowledged—that's natural. In the end, what is it that you want to be remembered for, just being loud or because you had something to say?

Experiment: The next time you're among your peers, look around and see who's commanding all the attention. Once you've found that person, listen. See if they're just talking loud or if they really have something to say.

69. Take your time.

For the length of days, and long life, and peace,
shall they add to thee. (Proverbs 3:2 KJV)

- Don't rush yourself or wish your life away! Learn to enjoy the process of living. Take time to enjoy a sunset, a sunrise, a moonlit night, or a walk on the beach. Make time to enjoy all that life has to offer.

We are a generation of people who want everything now (the "microwave age"). We no longer want to cook, so we stop by the drive-thru on the way home. On the rare occasion that we are cooking at home, it usually involves "zapping" something in the microwave.

Writing a letter using pen and paper is a thing of the past. With the advent of email delivered to your desktop, who wants to wait for a letter in the mailbox?

We can no longer wait to get home to make a call; we can and do call from our car or wherever we are. Have a cell phone! (I have one. I never leave home without it! ☺)

We're moving too fast. Have you said that there is not enough time or where did the time go? In order to make the most of what life has to offer, we must take time to enjoy it. We must seek the wisdom and love of God and then share it. Take time for God.

70. Tell the truth.

> *And ye shall know the truth, and the truth shall make you free. (John 8:32 KJV)*

- Poll your friends: ask them if they prefer the truth or a lie. Assuming they will say the truth, why do we lie so much and so freely?

If I got paid every time I heard this or said it to my children, what a paycheck I'd receive! ☺

Every time we have experienced an accusation that was not fair or true, this saying came to mind.

It's a reminder that if we hold fast to the truth, not reacting to every accusation, the truth comes out when all is said and done.

71. The bigger they are, the harder they fall.

> *No one is respected unless he is humble; arrogant people are on the way to ruin. (Proverbs 18:12 GNT)*

- Do not get caught up in your accomplishments and whom you know.

What are the most memorable events of the past year to you? I recently watched a show that talked about various divorces, people on drugs and arrested for carrying drugs, driving while under the influence, and theft. These stories were all about people who tended to think they were larger than life, who, when seen on the street, would be afraid you might want something. They were all splashed across the headlines, as if your very life depended on knowing about the most intimate details of their lives. I wonder if any of them ever heard of you or me. I wonder why "we" never make the headlines. Could it be that we are not as interesting?

Try this:

Eliminate all negative news from your life for thirty days: the newspaper, TV, and radio. Once that thirty-day period is up, I would be willing to bet that you will have a different opinion of what is important and what's not.

72. The blind leading the blind.

Let them alone: they be blind leaders of the blind. And if the blind lead the blind, both shall fall into the ditch. (Matthew 15:14 KJV)

- This is an example of a person who does not know what they are doing but is persuasive enough to get others to follow them.

Momma did not mean that I could not physically see. What she meant was that I had a lack of knowledge or understanding about a certain situation.

A group decides to take a trip; one person says they know where they're going and how to get there. However, once the trip gets underway, they end up getting lost. The tough thing is that everyone depended on that one person and didn't take the time to research the directions for themselves. A perfect example of "the blind leading the blind."

73. The darkest hour is just before dawn.

I will bless the Lord who counsels me; he gives me wisdom in the night. He tells me what to do. I am always thinking of the Lord; and because he is near, I never need to stumble or to fall. (Psalm 16:7–8 TLB)

- Problems always seem the worst just before your "breakthrough" happens. While waiting for that breakthrough seems like forever, once it happens, it then seems like it happened overnight.

This, of course, has nothing to do with physical light and darkness. It has everything to do with us when we "feel" we have nowhere to turn. When we've done just about all we could and our situation appears hopeless, that's just about the time the dawn of a new day arrives. It is at this time that we are open and receptive to hear a word from God. Sometimes, He has to allow us to break before we can be "fixed."

Here are a few of those dusk-till-dawn times:

- The bills are all past due, and an unexpected check arrives in the mail that covers all the bills that are due.
- A potential transplant patient gets a suitable donated organ, days before all hope is gone.
- Baseball: Your team is at bat and down by one point. It is the bottom of the ninth inning with two outs. The count is three balls and two strikes with one man on base. The batter hits a home run. Your team wins!

74. The grass is always greener on the other side.

The grass withers, the flowers fade, but the Word of God shall stand forever. (Isaiah 40:8 TLB)

- We always want what someone else has, never satisfied with what God has blessed us with. We fail to take thought of how that person obtained what it is that they have.

- To become a successful entrepreneur requires giving unselfishly of oneself. You must know all aspects of the business. From the outside, you see only the finished product. On the inside, you can experience financial, emotional, physical, and mental stress and strain. Sleepless nights and lots of long hours away from your family are the rule rather than the exception.
- A happy well-adjusted family requires quality time and for the parents to forget words like *I*, *me*, and *mine*. Onlookers don't see the late nights sitting up with sick kids or the endless hours spent carpooling.
- To maintain a 4.0 GPA, you must study and give up the party life.
- Top athletes get there by hours and hours of practice. All we see are the "big bucks."

If you want it, you can have it, just not someone else's. If you are in line with the Word of God, "ask and you shall receive."

75. The Lord would not put more on you than you can handle.

For my yoke fits perfectly, and the burden I give you is light. (Matthew 11:30 NLT)

- Tests are meant to strengthen us. Instead of seeing them as trials, see them as opportunities. This is a chance to exercise our faith so we can move to the next level in Christ.

Without a test, how do we know what our limitations are? How do we know the depth of our faith?

No matter the situation, God has given us the perfect example to follow. All we have to do is ask ourselves, "What would Jesus do?"

76. The main thang is the plain thang, and the plain thang is the main thang.

> *And the Lord answered me, and said write the vision, and make it plain upon tables, that he may run that readeth it. (Habakkuk 2:2 KJV)*

- It's okay to use everyday words to explain what you believe, so that everyone will understand.

This saying truly speaks for itself. I think of Pastor Otis Lewis Sr. when I hear this saying. I can recall him saying it, in some form, when there were scriptures that were controversial and several members voiced their take on what they meant. He would intervene with this saying in some form. The gist of it is what's important stands by itself and needs no explanation or debate—it's plain and simple. If we have a personal relationship with God, no one has to explain the meaning of Scripture. When we have a question, all we need do is ask God. He will make sure that it makes sense to us.

77. The one who screams the loudest is the one who's guilty.

A man is known by his actions. An evil man lives an evil life; a good man loves a godly life. (Proverbs 21:8 TLB)

- When we are under God's covering, He justifies us. We should let the facts speak for themselves.

- Take a moment and reflect on the times when you've seen a movie and several people, together as a group, were accused.

Usually, the first one to say "I didn't do it" or "I was not here when it happened" or attempt to offer an explanation of what "did not" happen is usually the culprit or knows more than anyone else about what did happen.

78. The proof is in the pudding.

To them he presented himself alive after his passions by many infallible proofs, being seen of them forty days, and speaking of the things pertaining to the kingdom of God. (Acts 1:3 KJV)

- True acceptance of anything takes place when it becomes reality to you, when you can verify it by taste, touch, smell, sight, or sound.

It's not necessary to get defensive about your work, life, or family. (I do sometimes—just human, I guess.) As Christians, we're supposed to exercise our faith. When we exercise our faith, we put ourselves in a right relationship with God. We become examples to the world of what Jesus would do.

If we are living a spirit-filled life, following the principles of God, the battle is no longer ours; it's the Lord's.

79. The rich get richer, and the poor get poorer.

"Yes," the king replied, "but it is always true that those who have, get more, and those who have little, soon lose even that." (Luke 19:26 TLB)

• Eagles soar with other eagles. Rarely, if ever, do you see a loser in the winner's circle.

Thoughts to ponder:

- Why do we buy dinner for those who can afford to buy their own?
- Why do we give gifts to those who do not need them (especially at Christmas)?
- Why is it when you have little or no credit, you cannot find anyone to make you a loan or give you a credit card? Finally, when you do get that first card, everybody and his or her momma send you a preapproved card in the mail.
- Why is it that stars rarely pay for the "use" of jewelry, gowns, etc.?

80. Think before you leap.

A wise man is cautious and avoids danger; a fool plunges ahead with great confidence. (Proverbs 14:16 TLB)

- Take time to consider the alternatives before you make your final decision.

There have been many times when I was anxious and, before I thought out a clear plan, I agreed to be or do something that later turned out unwise for me or others. If I had simply used some time to think and form a plan, it would have worked out for my good.

- Are you satisfied with your career, or did you take the first job that came along?
- Did you take time to hear from the Lord on your choice of a mate, or did you settle?
- If you had "it" (whatever "it" is) to do over again, would you make the same choice?

Take time to plan your work. Then you can work your plan. Consult God before you make your decisions. Then, make all your leaps, "leaps of faith!"

81. This is going to hurt me more than it hurts you.

All this I have seen, and applied my heart unto every work that is done under the sun: there is a time wherein one man ruleth over another to his own hurt. (Ecclesiastes 8:9 KJV)

• Correction hurts the parent first because it "feels" like failure. It hurts the child, which also hurts the parent all over again.

Most of us can say, "If I had a dollar for every time I heard my momma say that saying."

As kids, we had no idea what our mothers meant when they said that. All we knew was that we were the ones being punished.

How could the same person who said they loved me administer punishment?

What I understand now is that it was because of their love (and my offense) that I was punished.

As a mother, I understand that it was my spirit that hurt when I had to use physical discipline on my children. Although my children were crying (literally), as their mother I was also crying, inwardly.

As parents, we must set limits for our children. In doing so, we help to ensure their survival. We are helping to shape their personalities and giving them coping skills for their future. We do this so that they will be able to take care of themselves and so they will become productive members of society (and so they will move out!). ☺

82. This too shall pass.

Heaven and earth will pass away, but my words will not pass away. (Matthew 24:35 KJV)

- The sun follows rain, and joy follows pain. Just hold on.

No matter how difficult things are, this saying has always given me hope.

Whenever it has taken change a long time to come about or when it seemed that bad became worse and then worst, I could hear this saying in my thoughts: "It will pass after all. Nothing lasts forever."

83. Treat others the way you want to be treated.

Instead, be kind to each other, tenderhearted,
forgiving one another, just as God has forgiven you
because you belong to Christ. (Ephesians 4:32 TLB)

- Give someone a smile, a word of encouragement, or positive insight whenever possible.

This principle is easy to understand. However, the easiest principles are the most difficult to carry out.

Any and all of the following (just to name a few) can be stopped immediately, if only we would put ourselves in the other person's shoes:

- Cut in front of others (driving or parking).
- Ignore or look down on others for race or religious reasons.
- Lie to or about others.
- Rob, steal, or kill.

We would not want any of these things done to us, so why do we do them to others?

84. There are two sides to every story.

The first man to speak in court always seems right until his opponent begins to question him. (Proverbs 18:17 GNT)

- Everyone interprets a situation differently. When making a decision, it is best to hear all individuals who are involved.

How true this saying is to anyone who has witnessed an accident. The person on each side of the accident will report what they saw, and each report will be different. Until you have a personal encounter and give your observation and the person next to you gives theirs in your presence, only then will you have a personal perception.

There are two ways of looking at any situation. Do you see problems or possibilities? Which of the following would you choose?

- I see the glass as half full; or I see the glass as half empty.
- I see a job loss as an opportunity; or I see a job loss as a failure.
- I see writing a book as an opportunity; or I see writing a book as too much work.

85. Troubles don't last always; or there's light at the end of the tunnel.

And the Lord shall help them, and deliver them: he shall deliver them from the wicked, and save them, because they trust in him. (Psalm 37:40 KJV)

- As hard as this may seem, we must remember that we are not the first, nor will we be the last, to experience pain and hard times. Remain prayerful and seek God.

As a child and as an adult, when something is troubling me, I discuss it with my mother. Often her response has been this saying.

I believe what she is saying is that the situation you are in may seem as though it would last a time, but it's not going to last forever—it will end at some point.

86. Wait 'till you have children; or I hope your kids turn out just like you.

Children, obey your parents in the Lord: for this is right. (Ephesians 6:1 KJV)

- Each generation, during the teenage years, challenges their parents in some way. The unfortunate thing for the child is a lack of understanding of what it takes to be a parent. Hence, "wait 'till you have children" becomes a very appropriate response on many occasions.

Parents all around the world have most likely used this saying at least once or twice. Maybe it was during the "I know everything" teenage years or the "I'm grown. I'm in college" years. Whatever the occasion, the satisfaction comes when the child becomes a parent.

As children, we have a tendency not to listen to the wisdom that comes from our parents. We think they could have never experienced anything like what we are experiencing. What we don't know at that age is that the player may change, but the game remains the same.

With this saying, our parents were just trying to give us a "heads-up" on life's realities. They were trying to tell us that someday we would be parents and would experience similar situations with our children.

87. Walk the walk; talk the talk.

Another reason for right living is this: you know how late it is; time is running out. Wake up, for the coming of the Lord is nearer now than when we first believed. (Romans 13:11 TLB)

- Let your life be an example of what is good and right before God.

What kinds of examples are we setting?

- Managers/supervisors/bosses
  Do you demand of your staff things that you would not do?
- Health-care providers
  Are you educating your patients on the benefits of healthy living but not applying the same principles in your own life?
- Parents
  Are you telling your teens the value of abstinence but you have a live-in "friend"?

If we expect others to do as we say/suggest, we must first be willing to "set" the example or "walk the walk" that we talk.

88. Waste not; want not.

Because the Lord is my Shepherd, I have everything I need! (Psalm 23:1 TLB)

- When things are good, do not overspend.

- Have you ever experienced a bankruptcy? You live in the nicest house and drive the nicest car and have clothes in the closet with price tags on them all while living paycheck to paycheck?
- Have you ever argued with a spouse or loved one and something tragic happened before you got a chance to say, "I'm sorry"?
- Have you ever repeated a class that was free the first time, but you had to pay for it the second time (summer school)? Why? Because you played around during the year.
- Ever spent more time with things and friends than with God?

So much wasted time we can never get back. Let's start today using our time wisely.

89. We plan; God smiles.

> *We can make our plans, but the final outcome is in God's hands. (Proverbs 16:1 TLB)*
> *A man's heart deviseth his way: but the Lord directeth his steps. (Proverbs 16:9 KJV)*

- Difficulty, pain, and trouble usually follow decisions that did not include God.

- I always thought I'd get a job and take care of my mom. After all, she put her life on hold and took care of me. We would continue to live in "Small Town, USA," and life would be good. I thought it would be the right thing to do. (Little did I know that Mom had other plans.)
- I thought I'd never leave Florida (the Sunshine State). Who would willingly give up all that sunshine? (It's been many years since I resided there.)

Notice how the word *I* has been used? Nowhere in those examples did I mention God. We must continually go to God in prayer with our wants and desires. It should be His choice for our lives, not our selfish wants and desires.

90. What goes around comes around; or you reap what you sow.

> *And let us not be weary in well doing for in due season we shall reap, if we faint not. (Galatians 6:9 KJV)*
>
> *Don't be misled; remember that you can't ignore God and get away with it: a man always reap just the kind of crop he sows! (Galatians 6:7 TLB)*

- The way you treat others often determines how others will treat you.
- Be aware of what you dish out. That is the same thing that's coming back to you!

This saying is so appropriate for those times when we can't understand how some people excel at everything. Yet, others seem to fail at everything they attempt. Whether good or bad, we will receive our due. Even when it seems that we aren't having our time to shine, if we continue and keep the faith, we will have our time.

- Gardeners, what happens when you have good ground and weather and you tend and water your crops properly? You expect to see a good harvest.
- Cooks, what happens when you have all the correct ingredients prepared properly? You expect a delectable edible.
- Employees, you have excellent time and attendance all year, as well as an excellent evaluation. You expect to see a raise, don't you?
- This is for all of us: if we take care of our body, it will take care of us!

If you were to change any of the variables in the examples, the outcome would also change.

Be aware of what you dish out. That is the same thing that's coming back to you!

91. What you do in the dark will come to the light; or the truth will come to the light.

> *Therefore whatsoever ye have spoken in darkness shall be heard in the light; and that which ye have spoken in the ear in closets shall be proclaimed upon the housetops. (Luke 12:3 KJV)*

- Plans made in secret and carried out at night are short-lived. When you least expect it, your secret surfaces. Only then will you realize someone was observing you while you were sneaking around.

We "tell" on ourselves, because our behavior changes when we are doing something that is new to us. Parents, take note: some of these behaviors apply to teenagers as well as adults. We have even given this behavior a name for adults, "midlife crisis." Whatever you call it, watch for the following signs:

- Unexplained phone calls.
- He/she leaves the room when receiving "certain" phone calls.
- He/she lowers their voice during a call.
- Developing new friends or relationships that you are not a part of.
- A completely different style of dress.
- Coloring the gray or styling the hair completely different.
- Unexplained absence.
- Unexplained receipts.
- Missing money.

We are only kidding ourselves when we do any of the above things (for the wrong reasons). We may feel that we are smart enough to cover all the basis, but no matter how much you cover it, someone always sees you. What's done in the dark will come to the light.

92. What's good for the goose is good for the gander.

For there is no difference between Jew and the Greek: for the same Lord over all is rich unto all that call upon him. (Romans 10:12 KJV)

- There should be "one" set of rules for everyone. Race, sex, or money should not affect the way you treat people or are treated.

Some people think they should be the one making all the decisions and be in control or have things their way all the time.

What I find amazing is that as long as it's them living large, everything's all right. As soon as things aren't going so well, they want everyone to stop and take notice of their problem.

Examples:

- How does a robber feel when they get robbed?
- Jokes are always funny until the joke is on you.
- War is okay if you do not have to participate or if it is in another country.
- It's okay for you to cut someone off, but how do you feel when someone cuts you off?

We all have experienced some form of double standards.

93. What you see is what you get.

Different kinds of fruit trees can quickly be identified by examining their fruit. (Matthew 7:17 TLB)

- If it looks like a duck, walks like a duck, and quacks like a duck, it is a duck.

I must preface this by saying that we have some truly devious people in our lives who never show us who they really are. This saying does not apply to them.

- Would you buy a Volkswagen and, once you got it home, expect it to be a Ford?
- Do you buy chicken, thinking that after it is prepared it will be steak?

Why is it that we see life as it is but expect something other than what it is we see?

Before you tie the knot (get married):

- If she likes to shop, she will shop even more, this time with your money.
- If she doesn't cook before marriage, odds are that she will not cook once she's married.
- If he likes sports now, it will not change later.
- If he's controlling now, it'll be worse later.

Bottom line (for most things), "What you see is what you get."

94. Where there is a will, there is a way.

The hope of the righteous shall be gladness: But the expectation of the wicked shall perish. (Proverbs 10:28 KJV)

- When you want something with all your heart, seek God.

To do anything, you have to determine or decide to do it. Look back over your life and consider when things did not work for you. Could it be that you did not want them to? (By doing all you were supposed to.)

Sometimes you may require assistance, but once you decide to "do a thing," you get it done, don't you?

You may have accomplished your goal, maybe by working two jobs, going back to school, or studying or practicing for endless hours. The end result: you had the will, and you got your way.

95. You can please some of the people some of the time, but you can't please all of the people all the time.

> *Does this sound as if I am trying to win man's approval? No indeed! What I want is God's approval! Am I trying to be popular with men? If I were still trying to do so, I would not be a servant of Christ. (Galatians 1:10 GNT)*

- Our walk with Christ will not always be popular with our friends and family. Our priority should be pleasing God.

Whatever we do at home or at work should be done in the name of the Lord. Pray to ensure that your choices are pleasing to God, and don't worry about what anyone else thinks. After all, if God is pleased, who can complain?

96. You can't teach an old dog new tricks.

And said, "Unless you turn to God from your sins and become as little, you will never get into the Kingdom of Heaven." (Matthew 18:3 TLB)

- In general, we are reluctant to "change," to try new ideas. Why? FEAR (false evidence appearing real) of the unknown. *Get over it!*

We all know this is true—although I personally welcome change when it proves to be beneficial. The bottom line is that when we learn something and do it that way for many years, resistance is natural.

It's not that we can't learn the new way; change affects our comfort level and is replaced by resistance. Resistance is often the mask of fear.

97. You can catch more flies with honey than with vinegar.

Pleasant words are as sweet as an honeycomb, sweet to the soul, and health to the bones. (Proverbs 16:24 KJV)

- It is easier to get what you want when you are kind and humble, rather than when you aren't.

- Are you more apt to smile if someone smiles at you first vs. someone who does not respond?
- Are you more likely to say hello when you know the person will say hello to you vs. the person who looks away?
- Are you willing to share, or do you keep everything for yourself?

98. You can convince a fool of his will, and he will give his consent still.

> *Even if you beat a fool half to death, you still can't beat his foolishness out of him. (Proverbs 27:22 GNT)*

- Those who are knowledgeable often take advantage of people who lack knowledge and understanding.

So many times I have heard this saying; only through maturity have I come to understand it. It simply means that some people can talk others into doing things that appear on the "up and up," only to discover that they were misused. They participated in something that, if they had a better understanding, they would not have been a part of.

99. You never miss your water until your well runs dry.

For the scriptures declare that rivers of living water shall flow from the inmost being of anyone who believes in me. (John 7:38 KJV)

- We often take life, friends, and our parents for granted. It is not until that a parent's health begins to fail or that friend is no longer around that we realize their value in our lives.

Hey, you got it going on! Everything is going right in your world. Then "tragedy strikes."

- There's a job loss:
  You've been downsized or rightsized right out of the door.
- Sickness creeps in:
  Remember "I'm gonna start that diet tomorrow" or "I'm gonna join a gym as soon as I get some time." The results of waiting are either being overweight, hypertensive, or diabetic.
- Death strikes:
  You lose the person in your life whom you've taken for granted, such as your mother, mate, or best friend.

If you have never been in any of these situations, congratulations! If I were you, I would say a special thank you to God for His grace. Those of us who have experienced them will tell you not to take one minute of any day for granted. Especially, do not take anyone who means something to you for granted.

Say you're sorry or just pick up the phone and say hello and reestablish a friendship. Don't wait. Do it now while you have time.

100. You'll have to sleep in the bed you made.

He will be severely punished, for though he knew his duty he refused to do it. (Luke 12:47 TLB)

- Ultimately, we are responsible for *our own actions*.

- Ever quit a job based on a "promise" from someone offering you a higher salary? Once you did, you found out that it was not all it was supposed to be. Not only did you not get that job but you couldn't go back to your old job.
- When is the last time you spent more than you should have, with no visible means to pay the bill?
- Some of us have to learn the hard way, by making our own mistakes. So, parents, after you have done all you were supposed to by teaching your kids good morals and values, let them go. Allow your children the opportunity to figure some things out for themselves; just let them know that you will always love and support them.

101. You're getting too big for your britches; or the ones you meet on your way up are the same ones you meet on the way down.

> *It is better to get your hands dirty—and eat, than to be too proud to work—and starve. (Proverbs 12:9 TLB)*

- *Do not misjudge your own self-worth.*

"You have now arrived!" Wouldn't you like to hear those words in reference to your finances, as well as your personal life? Let's say you have "arrived." Now what? Do you reach back and help your "brother," or do you move on with your newfound circle of friends?

- Are you "the" star athlete, performer, doctor, or lawyer? Once you made it, did you try to help anyone else?
- Have you become wealthy and now you can no longer be bothered with those you "used" to know?

In either of these instances, and in many others, my momma would say, "You're getting too big for your britches." She would finish by saying, "The same ones you met on the way up will be the same ones you'll meet on your way back down."

About Sharon

S haron is biblically focused on her faith, believing in the loving Father, God; the living Son, Jesus; and the comforting Holy Spirit.

Sharon attributes her achievements as the direct result of a personal relationship with God.

Sharon's proudest achievements are the many roles she has been gifted with, which include being a daughter, sister, mother (three daughters), and wife.

Sharon is a Licensed Master Social Worker with over forty years of experience in providing direct service in the community and in management.

Sharon is blessed to share life with her daughters and Henry, a kind, generous, and loving husband, as well as being thankful for a small circle of girlfriends, who have been supportive and forgiving and blessed her with their love and their presence for many years.

Sharon is thankful to her mama as she heard her each time she told her a wise saying.

About Carolyn

C arolyn is the fourth of five children. From childhood she was known to be tenacious and fiercely loyal to family and friends.

One of her mother's wishes was for her children to graduate college. Carolyn fulfilled this dream of her mom's and one of her own, to serve her country in the military.

Born and raised in Florida, Carolyn has also spent time in Denver, Atlanta, and Korea. She has one son, and they both call Michigan home.

Some of the many influences in her life were Mrs. Roberta who shared her home on weekends from college and the Silver Foxes, who were "living" examples of Christian women.

It goes without saying that Momma Dot and Momma Noon are the inspiration from whence this book came. Without them, she would not be able to tell you what Momma Said.